Discover Gems

by Victoria Marcos

© 2012 by Victoria Marcos
ISBN: 9781623957032
eISBN: 9781623957049
Images licensed from Fotolia.com
All rights reserved.
No portion of this book may be reproduced
without express permission of the publisher.
First Edition
Published in the United States by Xist
Publishing
www.xistpublishing.com
PO Box 61593 Irvine, CA 92602

Diamonds are the hardest gems in the world.

They are formed about 100 miles beneath the Earth's surface at very high temperature and pressure.

They are used as cutting and polishing tools.

Sapphires are a variety of corundum. They are the third-hardest gems in the world, tied with rubies.

They are often used in scientific instruments, watch parts, and special high-tech equipment.

Although blue is their most common color, they can be various shades of gray and even colorless.

Rubies are also a variety of the corundum family. They get their color from the element chromium.

The brighter red and more colorful the ruby the more valuable it is. They can also be pinkish, purplish or brownish.

Rubies are almost as hard as the very rare, second-hardest gem, moissanite.

7

8

Emeralds are from the beryl family of minerals.

They have been mined by Egyptians since 1500 BC.

Although emeralds are found all over the world, most come from Colombia.

Morganite, also known as "pink beryl" is a rare gem in the beryl family of minerals.

Pure beryl is colorless. It gets its color from impurities that enter the gem when it is formed.

11

12

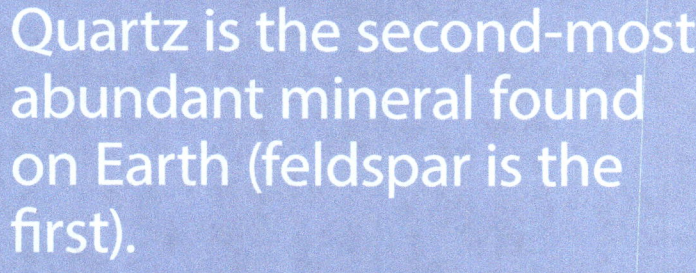

Quartz is the second-most abundant mineral found on Earth (feldspar is the first).

It often forms inside of hollow rocks and has an outer layer of agate.

Quartz is also called "rock crystal". There are many different colors of quartz, including black and colorless.

Quartz was the most-commonly used gem in ancient times to make jewelry and carvings.

Citrine quartz is found in colors ranging from pale yellow to brown.

It gets its color from iron impurities.

Its name comes from the Latin word "citrina" which means yellow.

When polished, citrine quartz becomes a beautiful gemstone that can be made into jewelry.

Although chalcanthite is blue in color it is a copper mineral.

Because of its beautiful color and crystals it is desired by many collectors.

Interestingly, it has a sweetly-metallic flavor.

21

Tourmaline is found in almost any color. Some gems may be one color on one end and another color on the other end or one color on the inside and another color on the outside.

Tourmalines were used by scientist in experiments over 100 years ago.

Agate is part of the chalcedony family of minerals and forms in open spaces in volcanic rock.

Agate can also be very colorful.

It was used by the ancient Greeks and Egyptians to make jewelry.

Onyx is part of the chalcedony family of minerals.

It is found in almost every color.

It contains white and black stripes. Most of the time, the solid black color is made artificially.

Onyx has a long history of being used as jewelry.

It has interesting colors and patterns.

The ancient Egyptians also used it for making bowls and pottery.

Fluorite is also known as "fluorspar" and is called "the most colorful mineral in the world".

Although it may not appear to be very colorful it glows in the dark under an ultraviolet light.

Obsidian is also found in open spaces of volcanic rock.

It is formed when lava cools very quickly and not many crystals form.

When broken, it forms very sharp edges.

Opals form in cracks of almost any rocks. They are found in a wide range of colors and patterns, but most opals are white in color.

Amber looks like a gem but it is actually fossilized tree resin.

It's worn as jewelry just as gems are.

It is also used in perfumes and as for healing in folk medicine.

Some children keep rock collections.

It's interesting to see the rock's different colors and patterns.

www.ingramcontent.com/pod-product-compliance
Lightning Source LLC
LaVergne TN
LVHW021600070426
835507LV00014B/1888